Railway Erie

Erie Railway Tourist

Railway Erie

Erie Railway Tourist

ISBN/EAN: 9783337193423

Printed in Europe, USA, Canada, Australia, Japan

Cover: Foto ©Andreas Hilbeck / pixelio.de

More available books at **www.hansebooks.com**

ERIE RAILWAY TOURIST

ERIE RAILWAY TOURIST

INTRODUCTION.

THE management of the Erie Railway Company presents the "Tourist" to its patrons, friends, and the general public, in this form, to introduce a more intimate and detailed knowledge of the beanties, advantages, and resources of its line.

The route of the Erie Railway is peculiarly rich among American railroads in the variety and extent of its scenery. In the following pages only a very few of the abounding landscapes of the route have been reproduced. The valley of the Neversink, as seen from the grade east of Port Jervis, rivals the view from the Starucca Viaduct ; and the panorama of beauty in the valley of the Delaware is continually interesting in the rapidly alternating glimpses of river, gaps, and mountains. Passing their summit, the pastoral beauties of the valleys of the Susquehanna and Chemung rivers widen into broader and more cultivated landscapes, reaching back to the receding mountains. Ascending again to the "Summit" which divides the waters between the ocean, the great lakes, and rivers, the Genesee and Alleghany rivers present new varieties of picturesque scenery, which will interest the observing business or pleasure traveler.

While the enjoyments of travel are enhanced by such prodigal attractions of Nature, which it is the desire to make more generally known, the route of the Erie Railway is also interesting in a consideration of its improvements and resources.

The following pages, therefore, state brief details of salient interest concerning the cities and towns along the line, and make general reference to the traffic resources, the development of which, upon a basis alike profitable to the transporter and the transported, it is believed will insure permanent prosperity to the Company, to the people, and to the enterprises tributary to the line.

To present these considerations more fully than before, this volume is issued ; and it is believed that a trip via the Erie Railway in its broad, richly-appointed cars, running over a track which challenges comparison for smoothness and safety, will be both pleasantly and profitably beguiled by a perusal of

"THE ERIE RAILWAY TOURIST."

"AT HOHOKUS."

EVERYBODY who can, leaves New York or its environs during the warm weather. Some whose purses are long, hie them to Long Branch, Newport, or Saratoga. But, by far the larger number, people of moderate means or quieter inclinations, eschew the haunts of fashion, and hurry away to some quiet nook in the country, or to some of the picturesque villages and towns which bestud Northern New Jersey and Orange county within a distance of a hundred miles from the metropolis.

In a work recently published by the Erie Railway Company, entitled, "Where shall we spend the Summer?" accurate information relating to all such points has been furnished gratuitously to the million. Let us here take a hurried glimpse of the hints—and they are good ones—which it offers those looking for a summer country boarding-place. It will surprise us, *en passant*, to note how the first hundred miles teem with cosy resorts of all varieties, from the modest farmhouse in the meadow-land, or the mountain cottage nestling under the shadows of wildest hillsides, to the summer hotels, fitted up with all the conveniences of city life. Here are Rutherford Park, with its fine summer hotel, and its splendid boating facilities on the Passaic; Clifton, overlooking the picturesque Lake Dundee; Ridgewood and Hohokus in the historic Paramus Valley; Suffern and Ramapo, with their good hotels and bracing mountain air; Cornwall and Newburgh nestling among the Highlands of the majestic Hudson; Greenwood Lake, surrounded by mountains, and with three first-class hotels facing it; Goshen, Florida, and Middletown, all of them delightful places right in the heart of the famous dairy region of Orange county, a land literally flowing with milk and honey; Seven-Spring Mountain, a picturesque resort near Monroe, and rendered attractive by an extensive and well-kept hotel; Guymard, another charming retreat on the Shawangunk mountain-side overlooking the Neversink Valley; Port Jervis, on the Delaware, almost shut in by high mountain-peaks, and most romantically located; Milford, eight miles from it, famed for its fine hotels, tiptop cookery, and pretty scenery;

WHILE there may be grander views on the line of the Erie Railway than that which the artist has sketched under the foregoing title, there are certainly none more lovely or alluring to the lover of nature. The view is taken looking eastward. On the right ascends a bold and thickly-wooded hillside; in the foreground is a heavy piece of masonry, spanning a watercourse some fifty or sixty feet below, while on the left, though unfortunately beyond the limits of the picture, stretching away from the base of the hill, the historic Paramus Valley, a glance at which from the car-window in passing discloses many points of interest. Close at hand is the former home of the beautiful Miss Prevost, who became the wife of Aaron Burr; farther off in the valley is the old Paramus Church, temporarily used as a prison-house by the British soldiery during the Revolution, while under the shadow of the green hills, bounding the valley's farther verge, is the country-seat of Jefferson, the famous comedian.

Monticello and White Lake, in the centre of the finest trout and game region in the State; Lake Mohonk, a beautiful body of water, lying 1,200 feet above the Hudson, is within five miles easy ride of New Paltz, on the Wallkill Valley Branch extending from Goshen. From this point or from Eagle's Cliff near by, may be gained a view that is surpassingly grand and impressive. Below lie the Rondout and Wallkill valleys; to the east winds the Hudson, beyond which may be traced the misty lines of the Green Mountains; while in the west, from the Alleghanies in the southwest to the Cone of Overlook in the north, the entire horizon is bounded by a piled-up wall of blue. So great has the popularity of this spot become, that it has been found necessary to enlarge the capacity of the hotel which is here situated, and which will now accommodate four hundred guests. The Overlook Mountain House, situated on Mount Overlook, a peak of the Woodstock Catskills, 3,860 feet high, is another attractive summer resort, and may be reached by the Wallkill Valley and New York, Kingston, and Syracuse Railways in connection with the Erie. From every room in the hotel, which accommodates five hundred guests, a magnificent view is obtained. The valley of the Hudson can be seen for one hundred miles, and the range of sight comprises also the Shawangunk, Catskill, and Berkshires. This has been a favorite resort for many years, and is visited annually by some of the most noted men in the country. All these make up the more prominent summer resorts to which, in every succeeding season of warm weather, long trains of city-tired passengers hasten by way of the Erie Railway. Then, in imagination, fill in the chinks of the picture with a thousand-and-one farmhouses — out-of-the-way places, but clean, attractive, and hospitable, where one in the dog-days may idle, read, sleep, eat, ride, and fish to his heart's content. Imagine all these, we say, and you gain some idea of the extent of annual travel from New York to local summer resorts on the Erie Railway.

THE HOME OF THE TROUT.

In its season there is no finer sport than trout-fishing; and no region in the vicinity of New York abounds in streams more replete with the "spotted beauties," than Pike and Wayne Counties in Pennsylvania, and Sullivan County in New York, all of which places are tributary to, and may be reached within a few hours by taking the trains of the Erie Railway to Port Jervis, the western terminus of the Eastern Division.

STONY BROOK GLEN.

About two miles from Dansville, the southern terminus of the Dansville and Mount Morris Branch of the Erie Railway, is the charming Glen of this name. As a resort for pleasure-seekers and Picnic and Excursion parties, it possesses many attractions, and is growing steadily in popular esteem. Its proximity to the celebrated Avon Springs commands for it a very liberal patronage from the visitors at that resort, while its convenience of access from the city of Rochester, acquires for it a name and fame in the western part of the State, worthy of special mention.

ROCK CITY.

Six miles from Salamanca, on the Western Division of the Erie Railway, is the wonderful and interesting place of this name. The peculiar formation of the rocks which here abound, and their immense size and unlimited number, excite the curiosity and astonish the hundreds of visitors who include a trip to this place in their round of annual Excursion tours.

THROUGH TRAVEL BY THE ERIE RAILWAY.

POSSIBLY there is no better gauge by which to measure the immense through travel which passes over the Erie Railway during any given period, than the number of the sleeping and drawing-room coaches which is daily sent out from the depot at Jersey City for each of the prominent Western cities. Time was, and not very long ago either, when to travel a hundred miles or so in the same railway coach was considered no small achievement; but this sinks into insignificance when we see daily departing from the Jersey City terminus of the line palatial Pullman coaches, each destined for some one of the principal cities in the West. Here, for instance, is one in which the traveler, without alighting, may be carried to Buffalo and Niagara Falls; another which crosses the Great Suspension Bridge, and goes on over the Great Western Railway of Canada to Detroit; another which continues on over the same route via the Michigan Central to Chicago; another which runs through by way of the Atlantic and Great Western Railway to Cleveland; another which carries its passengers, by the same road and without change, to Cincinnati; and last, but by no means least, a sixth coach which pauses not until it has crossed the Father of Waters, and landed its voyagers in the great city of St. Louis.

No amount of experience or habit, however much it familiarizes us with American travel, can ever serve to render commonplace to the thoughtful observer the grandeur of such a scheme as this, which daily sends out its coaches to cross half a continent. Nor less worthy of admiration and remark are the interiors of the coaches themselves. The upholsterer and the car-builder have combined to render them moving palaces, in which, by day or by night, the traveler may be surrounded with all the luxurious appointments of a first-class hotel. And thus it is that modern railway travel has been divested of its tedium and inconveniences, and a ride over the Erie Railway rendered an event pleasant enough to be remembered for a lifetime.

PARROTT FURNACES AT GREENWOOD.

THE Parrott Furnaces at Greenwood give the passenger, as he is whisked by them, a suggestive hint of the activity and enterprise which have developed themselves even here in the wild passes of the Ramapo Mountains. Here were forged, in the last century, the great chains which were used to obstruct navigation at West Point; and here to-day are manufactured the materials for the Parrott guns, which have spoken for themselves so loudly in every quarter of the globe.

But it is at night, when darkness has come down over field and forest, that the traveler, in passing Greenwood, looks out upon these furnaces to see them in their most striking phase. The lurid light, flashing from the glowing fiery portals, throws weird reflections and shadows far out upon the darkened mountain side, revealing here and there the pygmy forms of the workmen hurrying, imp-like, hither and thither at their toils. Great volumes of black smoke belch forth from the towering funnels and chimneys, only to be caught suddenly by the mountain breezes and carried far away out of vision. Some striking scene from Doré and Dante, seems to have been suddenly pictured upon the darkness of night. And yet, ere the surprised and wistful gazer has realized the vision, it has gone, and he looks out again only upon darkness.

GREENWOOD IRON-WORKS AT NIGHT.

ORANGE LAKE.

ONE of the most picturesque sheets of inland water in the country, is situated six miles west from Newburgh, and may be reached in a few hours, via the Erie Railway. Its attractions for tourists and those fond of aquatic and piscatorial sports are numerous, and will repay a visit.

BLOODED STOCK.

As famous as is Orange County for its milk and butter, no less renowned is it for its blooded stock, specimens of which may be seen in almost every part of the country. To have paid more than a thousand dollars a few years ago for a horse that could trot a mile under three minutes, was considered an exorbitant price, and the horse that could perform this feat was considered quite a phenomenon; while to-day there are hundreds of horses raised in Orange County, that can trot a mile in less than three minutes, and very many for which their owners would promptly refuse twenty-five thousand dollars.

Chester, Goshen, and Middletown, in Orange County, have the finest stables of thoroughbred-stock, which are visited weekly by admirers of fine stock from every section of the country.

The Erie Railway passes through these beautiful villages.

VISITORS to the United States, and Americans returning from abroad, are met on their arrival at the port of New York by courteous and experienced agents of the Erie Railway Company, who furnish them with all desired information respecting the route, its connections, rates of fare, time-tables, etc.

FALLS ON THE RAMAPO.

THIS lively stream, one of the chief tributaries of the Passaic, has its rise in Orange Co., New York, whence it flows southward into New Jersey, uniting its waters with those of the Pequannock at Pompton, and a few miles farther with those of the former river. At no point in its career, however, does it present a more striking or picturesque aspect than in the wild valley by which it finds its way through the mountain range which gives it its name. With a rapid fall, it furnishes, at various points, a splendid water-power for manufacturing purposes, while at others presenting numerous pretty cascades and bits of sylvan scenery such as the artist has presented in the engraving given herewith.

- - -

IT is at Lackawaxen that the Delaware and Hudson Canal, connecting the coal regions of Pennsylvania with the Hudson at Kingston, crosses the Delaware river, spanning it by an aqueduct, as represented in the accompanying engraving.

AQUEDUCT OF THE DELAWARE AND HUDSON CANAL AT LACKAWAXEN.

WHAT GIVES POPULARITY TO A RAILWAY?

1st. Good management; a strict regard to the comfort and safety of passengers.

2d. Low rates of fare, fostering and encouraging travel.

3d. Suitable equipment, with trains sufficient to accommodate all the business that offers.

4th. Regularity in the running of trains.

5th. Suitable eating-houses, at convenient points on the line.

6th. Variety and richness of scenery.

All these, and more which might be added, contribute to the well-earned success and popularity of the Erie Railway.

A SCENE ON THE DELAWARE.

The upper waters of the Delaware abound in scenery of the wildest and most picturesque description, the river banks at many points descending in precipitous abrupt cliffs of rock to the very water's edge, rendering the original construction of the railway through this valley a work of no ordinary difficulty. At other points the river has left deposits of soil along its margin, oases, as it were, in the desert of rock, where trees have grown, and cattle may find a pasture-ground. It is one of these latter spots that the artist has chosen to portray in the accompanying beautiful engraving.

THE OLD BRIDGE OVER THE DELAWARE—NARROWSBURG.

OLD BRIDGE OVER THE DELAWARE—NARROWSBURG.

Here the artist has sketched an old-fashioned country scene in one of the wildest portions of the Delaware Valley traversed by the Erie Railway. The old covered bridge is of a style frequently seen in that region, which, by the way, is the scene of many of the most stirring incidents in Fenimore Cooper's famous novel, "The Last of the Mohicans."

EMPLOYES OF THE ERIE RAILWAY.

In the service of the Erie Railway there are over 12,000 employes. From this some idea may be formed of the rapid growth and development of an enterprise which, in its inception, was regarded by the "knowing ones" as an undertaking involving the greatest pecuniary risk. "Small beginnings achieve great results;" and the Erie Railway of to-day, when contrasted with the "New York & Erie" of days agone, furnishes another illustration of the correctness of this trite old adage.

GREENWOOD LAKE

Is situated in Orange Co., within ten miles of Monroe, on the line of the Erie Railway, at which point stages connect twice daily for the lake.

As a summer resort it enjoys considerable distinction, owing to its proximity to the city, the variety of means of enjoyment which it offers, and the healthfulness and beauty of the locality.

PASSENGER AND FREIGHT EQUIPMENT.

There are owned and in use by the Erie Railway Company in the transportation of its passengers and freight, over five hundred engines, more than four hundred passenger, mail, baggage, and Express cars, (exclusive of Drawing-room and Sleeping coaches,) and about eleven thousand freight cars. A railway whose equipment is so great, and withal of the best and most approved patterns and finish, deserves to take rank among the leading passenger and freight thoroughfares of the country.

A SCENE ON THE DELAWARE NEAR CALLICOON.

SUBURBAN HOMES ON THE ERIE.

THE remarkable growth and development within the past ten years of the counties of New Jersey adjacent to, or within twenty miles of New York city, are to be ascribed, more than to any other cause, to the enterprise and liberality with which the various railways which traverse them are conducted. Before these railways were constructed it was considered impracticable for any one doing business in New York city to live elsewhere than on Manhattan Island, or possibly in Brooklyn or Jersey City. Now, on the other hand, thousands upon thousands of men in every sphere and avocation of metropolitan business life have their homes in New Jersey, and find them fully as easy of access as an up-town residence. Prior to 1860, the growth of New York exceeded greatly that of the seven neighboring counties of New Jersey, viz.: Bergen, Passaic, Essex, Hudson, Middlesex, Morris, and Union; but in that year their relative growth was as sixty-four to fifty-eight in favor of the latter, and this proportion had increased in 1870 to the enormous ratio of sixty to sixteen. At that time, the census showed a population of 942,292 in New York, as against 813,669 in 1860—and a population of 449,337 in the seven New Jersey counties, as against 287,876 in 1860. At the present time, of the 2,220,627 souls living in New York and a radius of forty miles around it, twenty-four and a quarter per cent. are residents of New Jersey.

In inviting and accommodating this class of daily suburban travel, the Erie Railway has displayed a far-seeing and liberal spirit. Its trains to local points are frequent and fast; its commutation rates so moderate as even to justify surprise. The result, however, has shown itself in a gratifying growth along the entire Eastern Division of the line. Where ten years ago were only farms and woods, villages and towns have sprung into existence as if by magic, while the sleepy hamlets of a decade ago have taken an infusion of new life, and fairly bristle with metropolitan activity. Every year hundreds more are finding their way out from the high rents and crowded quarters of New York to healthful and attractive homes on the line of the Erie Railway. Rutherford Park, Passaic, with its eight thousand inhabitants, Clifton, Lake View, overlooking the beautiful Dundee lake, Paterson, itself a great city of forty thousand, Hawthorne, Ridgewood, Hohokus, and Suffern, all teem with New York business men, who wisely prefer a ride to and from their homes in comfortable coaches to a tiresome jolt up and down town in crowded city horse-cars.

The same may be said of hundreds who dwell on the lines of the various branches of the Erie within twenty miles of New York; on the Newark and Paterson branch, which follows the romantic Passaic; on the Hackensack branch, which borders the river of the same name; and on the Northern Railroad of New Jersey, which, skirting the western slope of the Palisades, finds again an outlet to the Hudson at Nyack.

Further on up the main line too, at Turner's, Monroe, Goshen, Newburgh, Middletown, and Port Jervis, are to be found the homes of hundreds of wealthy New Yorkers, who, having passed the hurry and activity of life's noonday, find in these beautiful resorts, quiet homes from which they may yet conveniently visit New York whenever business demands. Year by year the exodus hitherward increases, and the day is certainly not distant when, for the first twenty-five or thirty miles of its route, the Erie Railway will traverse one continuous rural city, the creation in a great measure of its own liberality and enterprise.

* * *

THE ERIE RAILWAY FERRIES.

CONNECTING the lower part of New York city and its eastern and southern environs with New Jersey, is the Chambers street Ferry of the Erie Railway; and connecting the upper portion of the city with New Jersey is the Twenty-third street Ferry of the Erie Railway.

These two ferries are crossed annually by 5,000,000 people, thousands of whom transact business in New York, but reside on the Line of the Erie Railway; thousands are residents of Jersey City and its suburbs, while thousands seek these ferries in their passage between the Metropolis and the great West and South.

The number of boats run on these two ferries is six, of which four are in daily use, and two are held in reserve.

On the Chambers street ferry trips are made every fifteen minutes, and on the Twenty-third street ferry every half hour.

The advantages of having two ferries connecting New York with the Jersey City dépôt of the Erie Railway can not be overestimated. Many of the leading business houses of the Metropolis have removed from their old quarters "down town" to the vicinity of Twenty-third street, while nearly all of the principal hotels are located above Twenty-third street. The Twenty-third street ferry therefore facilitates communication with these houses and the upper portion of the city, and relieves the tedium of a trip through the crowded thoroughfares of the city by the ordinary means of conveyance—the city horse-cars.

The Chambers street Ferry communicates directly with the larger mercantile, banking, newspaper, and private and public institutions in the lower portion of the city, and thus accommodates a large and growing travel. Its convenience to the wharves of the principal lines of ocean, sound, and river steamers, also commands for it a very liberal patronage.

The Erie Railway, it will thus be seen, has admirably located ferries, as well as an unsurpassed route for communication between the East and the West.

A WATER TANK ON THE ERIE.

at which all express tr:
able hours to allot [p
tunity for refreshing th
there to be found at the
hurry and confusion w
invest [many of tho
of the Atlantic, or [.
of Mugby Junction
neat and handsome, s
in external appearance
nal appointments and
as to send every gues-
again feeling that is
equivalent in fare and
investment. The ha.
has, in fact, inaugura:
this regard ; and this :
less largely common :
route for travel to thos
pleasure compels to [
between the Atlanti-
States.

THE rapidity and voracity with which the iron horse quenches his thirst from one of these enormous goblets which, brimming full, await him at various intervals on his wild careering across the country, are all but incredible to those who have not seen him partaking. Parched and thirsty, he pauses for a moment or two to refresh himself with the cooling torrent which pours itself into his enormous jaws at a fearful rate, when lo! before apparently all the passengers have alighted or embarked, his thirst is slaked and he is off again.

NO "MUGBY JUNCTIONS" ON THE ERIE RAILWAY.

SOME recent wit has said that more crime results from empty stomachs than from vicious brains, and supplements it with the corollary that there is less virtue in morals than in beef and potatoes. Be this an exaggerated statement or not, one thing is certain—that a man's views of men and things in general depend a good deal upon whether he is hungry or no. He must be more than mortal who can deal gently with his fellow-creatures, or smilingly survey a lovely landscape, while experiencing the inward protest against that vacuum which nature is especially said to abhor. Therefore it will be admitted that there was consummate wisdom and forethought displayed in the arrangement which has provided at intervals along the line of the Erie Railway, commodious hotels or restaurants.

THE ERIE RAILWAY BAGGA

ONE of the greatest conveniences to Erie Railway, and one which elicits g tion, is the perfect and well-organized : delivery to and from its dépôts in Jer York.

Passengers purchasing tickets via in New York or Brooklyn, and desir removed to the dépôt, have now only t at the offices of the Company, when on their baggage and check it direct from to destination. This is a great desir away with the annoyance and loss of experienced by those who intrust the custody of indifferent and irresponsible panies.

Nor is the Erie Railway Baggage modation only to persons leaving, the c sengers are alike benefited by it, as he trains in the Jersey City dépôt, an age each car and takes up checks for bagga whatever part of New York or Brooklyn sent.

Passengers who have suffered from delivery of their baggage will appreciate of the Erie Railway Company to remed is generally regarded to be the most a railroad travel.

2

WHITE LAKE

This attractive summer resort, which has been for many years a favorite with the New York public, is situated in Sullivan County, near Monticello, which is connected with the main line of the Erie Railway by a Branch Railway from Port Jervis.

Its access is therefore rendered both easy and comfortable; and no wonder it is that during the hot and sultry days of July and August, it is thronged with visitors, who here find allurements for recreation and pleasure and a bracing mountain air of which but few localities can boast.

forty thousand inhabitants, and fairly points to its numerous locomotive works, its silk mills, and its numberless other varied industries in proof of its claims to be entitled the Manchester or the Lyons of America. No traveler who can spare a few hours should fail to stop over at Paterson and visit the Passaic Falls and the busy city about it.

AVON SPRINGS.

Avon Springs have for the last twenty years been more or less famed as a resort for invalids, their waters

GLIMPSE OF THE DELAWARE, NEAR CALLICOON.

PASSAIC FALLS.

In the heart of the great manufacturing city of Paterson, distant on the line of the Erie Railway only seventeen miles from New York, are the renowned Falls of the Passaic, second only to Niagara in grandeur and beauty. Indeed, these Falls in their peculiar configuration are said to have but one parallel, so far as known, on the globe, and that is the fall of the Mosi-oa-tunya, "Sounding Smoke," or Victoria Falls, on the Zambesi River in Africa, which, though vastly exceeding the Passaic cataract in height and volume, is so exactly its counterpart in all essential features that a bird's eye view of either might easily be mistaken for that of the other. The height of the Passaic Fall is seventy-five feet, furnishing, as may be supposed, in addition to the splendid scenery about it, a valuable water-power. It was this latter which induced Alexander Hamilton to establish here, in 1791, the manufacturing town of Paterson, which has grown to a city of

possessing many valuable healing properties. The Springs are located within a mile of the village of Avon, which is on the Rochester Division of the Erie Railway, and connected by two daily trains with New York.

ITHACA.

Of the many interesting and attractive Summer Resorts of easy access from New York, Ithaca is worthy of special mention. Its situation is at the head of Cayuga Lake, 270 miles from New York, and is reached in about ten hours, via the Erie Railway.

The scenery in the immediate vicinity of Ithaca compares favorably with that of Watkins Glen, and is regarded by many as equally sublime. The numerous Cascades and Falls which here present themselves in rapid succession, afford the Tourist some of the finest views of American scenery.

EAST AND WEST BRANCHES OF THE DELAWARE, NEAR HANCOCK.

THE SCENERY ON THE ERIE RAILWAY

ONE continued panorama, as varied as it is beautiful, greets the eye of the traveler by the Erie Railway from New York to either of its great western termini. It may, in fact, be questioned whether any other of the great lines of through travel in America, or even in the world, affords so many strikingly beautiful scenes, and such a variety of them withal, as are presented by this broad, double-tracked highway, extending in a majestic sweep through valley and meadow and mountain pass from the Hudson River to the Great Lakes and the Ohio River. Through the distance the eye of even the most unobservant is feasted with a succession of natural beauties which not but impress themselves vividly upon his mind main there long after the actual vision has — What stream in America more romantically beauti the Passaic, upon the wooded shores of which, its villas and lawns, the traveler looks down from the spanning its placid current? What grander tion of American enterprise and growth can be had the city of Paterson, with its busy shops and — Port Jervis, with its ceaseless roaring of railway and its immense coal traffic, and Binghamton, and Hornellsville, with their rapid development — *emporia*—all of them annually bringing to their b tor, the Erie Railway, increased rewards for its ben

Nor in man's handiwork alone does the trav the most to admire in traversing the line. In th passes of the Ramapo; the fertile and picturesqu scapes of that great dairy region, Orange County, an the giddy slopes of the weird Shawangunk M looking down upon the thickly populated valley Neversink, he will see ever new beauties, furnishi terial for ever deeper admiration. Or when the seemingly losing itself among the mountain which skirt the upper Delaware, shoots along th brink, overshadowed by giant hills which appear frowningly down upon this invasion of their dom there not a grandeur in the surroundings which bi ance to the tameness and routine of every-day exi Then, emerging from the hilly country, the passeng stretched out before him the widespread and pro farming region of Central New York.

Here he crosses the famed Starucca Viaduct, at which, in coming ages, the traveler will only gl wonder at the engineering skill and genius of on then come the fair regions watered by the Susqu the Chemung, and the Canisteo, all of them dotte farms and populated by thriving and intelligent co ties. From Hornellsville to Buffalo the scenery en a magnificent view of the Wyoming Valley, and still, at the Portage Bridge and the Falls of the C River, which here passes through a narrow, steep gorge, and takes three successive leaps to the t the valley below. But an hour or two's ride bey Niagara Falls, the fame of which is known the wor Or, continuing westward from Hornellsville, the ger traverses the historic regions of Southwester York; passes through the Cattaraugus and All Reservation, comprising several thousand acres, have been set apart for the use of, and are occup the Seneca Nation of Indians, of which tribe abo receive annuities from the Government.

dence, in princely style, with groves, lawns, terraces, fountains, and statuary, all so tastefully commingled as to at once strike the visitor with their beauty and arrangement. A visit to Eldridge Park should be an indispensable feature of a stay of even a day in Elmira.

STARUCCA VIADUCT.

One of the greatest engineering achievements on the entire route of the Erie Railway is the Starucca Viaduct pictured on the opposite page, which spans a great valley near the village of Susquehanna, Pa., by eighteen arches of solid masonry, each of them fifty feet in width. Its total length is 1,200 feet, its height 110, and its cost was $320,000. The roadway passes directly over the viaduct. In sunshine or in storm, by night or by day, amid the snows of winter or the leafy beauties of summer, this grand work stands out boldly upon the landscape about it, a tribute to the genius and energy of man, and a source of wonder and admiration to the traveler, by whom it is plainly visible from the car windows at either end of the long curve of which the viaduct forms about the centre. Many throughout the land are familiar with it as the most salient feature in that world-wide painting by Cropsey, entitled, "An American Autumn."

Farther on, connection is made with the Atlantic & Great Western Railway, which skirts the beautiful Chatauqua Lake, passes through the wonderful oil regions of Northwestern Pennsylvania, then the thickly populated farming regions of Northeastern Ohio, and ere he knows it, is at Lake Erie, in the great city of Cleveland; or, continuing southwestward, passes through the long line of populous towns in Central Ohio, and reaches in turn Dayton and Cincinnati without change of coaches since leaving the great metropolis. And throughout the entire distance the scene has been one of continuous and absorbing interest—a scene which the handiwork of the Creator and the artifice of man, though blended, have continuously vied to beautify and adorn.

- - -

ELDRIDGE PARK, ELMIRA.

Many visitors to Elmira avail themselves of the opportunity afforded by the liberality of one of its wealthy private citizens, to view one of the choicest bits of park and landscape gardening to be found in America. This, known as Eldridge Park, is the property of Dr. Eldridge, of Elmira, who, having amassed immense wealth, has laid out his estate, consisting of the grounds about his resi-

THE ERIE RAILWAY TELEGRAPH.

If additional facts were needed to show that the Erie Railway is a grand achievement, and well deserving the large and increasing patronage and popularity which it enjoys, by reason of the number and regularity of its trains, reference to its telegraph facilities should certainly serve the purpose. From statistics it appears that at the beginning of the present year there were in use 3,745 miles of wire, connected by 1,138 miles of poles. The number of operators required to do the business of the Company is about 350, and the number of telegraph stations or offices is over 200, of which 65 are open day and night.

With such an immense number of miles of wire under its control, operated by careful and experienced hands, it may readily be inferred that the business of the Erie Railway is something wonderful; and that to its telegraph facilities may safely be traced the uniform regularity in the running of trains.

THE CAULT A TRAITE.

WATKINS GLEN.

way, there is, it may safely be said, none save Niagara Falls, which will bear comparison with that wild and picturesque gorge which of late years has become such a favorite resort, and acquired such a fame among tourists under the title of Watkins Glen. It is reached by taking the Erie Railway to Elmira, 274 miles from New York, and thence, by another ride of twenty-two miles northward over the Northern Central Railroad. The adjacent village of Watkins is at the head of Seneca Lake, a beautiful body of water forty miles long and from two to four wide, and connected daily by steamers with Geneva. The Glen, which is in close proximity to the village, is, in brief, a vertical split or gorge some five or six hundred feet deep, in a bluff of solid rock, through which a stream passes in successive falls and other watery antics.

"So beautiful," says Appleton, "did the late Secretary Seward consider this sylvan retreat, that he brought the whole Diplomatic Corps to visit it on the occasion of that tour in which he showed them the wonders of this country." Then, as a resort, the Glen was not generally patronized or known, but now it is annually visited by thousands, and its hotels are among the best at any of the American watering places.

A ramble through Watkins Glen, even at the height of a summer noonday, is cool and delightful. Passing through a series of alcoves, stairways, and bridges, each ending in some delightful surprise, with some fresh beauty beyond it, one looks up at intervals from the darkened depths of the cleft in which he stands to see above—oh, how far above him!—the single little narrow strip of sky which reminds him of the accustomed sights of the outer world, and tells him he is not quite in fairy land. At some points, however, the commingling of waterfall, rock, turf, and foliage, makes up a scene which might well form a home for the Fauns and Dryads, and which never fails to elicit expressions of delight from even the most stolid observer.

From the summit of the mountain, too, may be had a superb view of Seneca Lake, the village of Watkins, and miles in extent of surrounding scenery. The whole picture is one of stirring interest and romantic beauty, and as the ascent of the mountain is easily accomplished, no visitor to Watkins Glen should rest satisfied until he has witnessed the unrivalled view which it affords.

WATKINS GLEN.

Among the natural beauties and curiosities to be found by the tourist in the regions traversed by the Erie Railway

THREE miles south of Watkins, near Seneca Lake, is the pretty village of Havana, the county town of Schuyler county, and, like Watkins, possessing within its borders rare natural attractions. The Glen is grandly picturesque, and includes some striking views, one of which, the Cathedral, is worth a long journey to see. The Springs, known respectively as "Cole's Spring" and the "Sanitarium," possess remarkable health-giving properties, and are so magnetically impregnated, that a knife-blade, after being held in the water a few moments, will attract to it small metallic substances. There are two good hotels at Havana Glen, and the Cook Academy, a well-organized institution of learning, formerly known as the People's College, occupies a commanding situation in the eastern part of the village. Havana Glen is reached by the same routes from New York and Philadelphia as Watkins.

THERE are many who every summer their vacation, and in seeking relaxation country life, but in being constantly in true keeping with our American spirit of listlessness. And it is to accommodate these years past the Erie Railway made arrangements with numerous connecting lines, to announce for sale, at reduced rates, a large cursion Tickets, embracing all points of interest, both on and off its main lines. The Erie Railway Company offers tickets that take you first to Watkins Glen, then to Seneca to Portage Falls, then to Niagara Falls, then Ontario, and down the magnificent St. Lawrence treal; thence down Lake Champlain to thence to Saratoga and Albany, and land via either Day or Night Line Steamer Hudson. Now, such a trip as this took to buy your ticket over each section of the route as you went along, was expensive and troublesome. But ent system, you buy your entire ticket in New York at a rate much less would otherwise be compelled to moreover, the privilege of stopping one of the prominent points that takes you. The points and routes ually in the trip here sketched were at random. But all summer resorts and beauty in New York, New England Canadas, are embraced in the series summer excursion tickets annually the Erie Railway Company.

In addition to these, another series offered for the benefit of those who one or two days of absence from the other duties at home. These tickets chaser to the Catskills, to Monticello some one of the hundreds of pretty one hundred miles of New York, a pleasant trip through the adjacent that, too, at a rate of fare consider that charged for ordinary local travel.

- - -

"ON TIME."

THE promptitude with which passengers on the Erie Railway have been year is deserving of commendation statement from the General Post office shows that, of the entire number of York of trains carrying the United the Erie Railway was from 13 to 37 of all other railroads for the first of the

ITINERARY OF THE ERIE RAILWAY.

NEW YORK TO NIAGARA FALLS BY DAYLIGHT.

Leaving New York from the foot of Twenty-third street, North River, at 8:45 A. M., or from the foot of Chambers street at 9 A. M., you are conveyed to the dépôt of the Erie Railway Company at Jersey City, directly opposite New York, from which trains are despatched at frequent intervals for all stations on the line, including Rochester, Buffalo, Niagara Falls, and all parts of the West and Southwest.

Your objective point being Niagara Falls, and your purpose being in leaving New York at either of the hours above named, to make the trip over the Erie Railway by daylight, in order to witness its magnificent scenery and the many objects of interest and beauty which have rendered its fame both enviable and world-wide, you provide yourself with tickets entitling you to an apartment or to a reserved chair in one of the Palace Coaches which accompany the Day Express train over the entire route.

The train being in readiness, you enter the Palace Coach, and are assigned by the porter in charge to whatever position in the coach is described on your tickets. Promptly at the advertised hour of departure (9:15 A. M.) a signal is given, the conductor announces "all aboard," and the train moves from the dépôt. In a few minutes you enter Bergen Tunnel, and are soon crossing the Hackensack meadows, when suddenly there appears in view the first station on your westward journey—Rutherford Park.

But you do not stop here. Onward you pursue your trip, crossing the Passaic river at Passaic Bridge, and passing the beautiful suburban towns of Passaic, Clifton, and Lake View, when you arrive at Paterson, N. J., a manufacturing city second only in importance to Newark, with which it is connected by a Branch railway 11 miles in length. From Paterson you continue your journey through the fertile and productive section of country in which are the cosy settlements of Hawthorne, Ridgewood, Hohokus, Allendale, Ramseys, and Mahwah, until you reach Suffern. The train does not stop, but you pause here to reflect how in years past the immense traffic of this great highway of travel (then known as the New York & Erie Railroad) radiated from this point to Piermont, on the Hudson river, 25 miles north of New York city, and accommodated itself to the facilities then furnished for communication with New York.

Leaving Suffern and glancing out of the window, you find yourself travelling through a valley of historic and romantic interest—he Ramapo—which is also the name of the next station. Following this are Sloatsburg, Southfields, and Greenwood, all of them healthful localities.

Turner's is next reached, and here the train makes a stop. You experience no sense of fatigue, but on the contrary feel invigorated and refreshed from the journey already accomplished, and while the train is not in motion you step upon the platform of the coach and survey the "situation." While admiring the beauty of the surrounding scenery, your attention is attracted to a Branch road which here intersects with the Main Line. This road runs to Newburgh, on the west bank of the Hudson river, passing the beautiful and attractive villages of Highland Mills, Cornwall, and New Windsor.

The train is again under motion and new scenes appear. You have arrived at Monroe, at which station stages connect with local trains for Greenwood Lake and the Seven-Springs Mountain, two very popular summer resorts. Soon you pass Oxford and reach Greycourt, from which place two Branch railways diverge, one extending to Warwick and the other to Newburgh, the latter being known as the "old road to Newburgh." It intersects with the new road from Turner's to Newburgh at a place called Vail's Gate.

Still under full headway the train hurriedly passes Chester, and in a few minutes brings you in partial view of Goshen, where it next stops. Aside from the notoriety which is attached to this place from being one of the oldest towns in Orange county, and withal one of the prettiest, it awakens in the traveller, who has read and heard of the fame of Goshen butter, (though he may never have become more familiar with it,) more than ordinary interest. As a place of summer resort Goshen offers peculiar attractions, its situation being in the heart of the most healthful portion of Orange county. A branch railway, 43 miles in length, extends from here to Kingston, on the Hudson river, passing through the charming villages of Montgomery, Walden, New Paltz, and Rosendale. A few miles from Kingston is the famous Overlook Mountain, of the Catskill range; and a few miles distant from New Paltz, by stage, is the delightful summer resort known as Lake Mohonk. A branch road of 12 miles also connects Goshen with Florida and Pine Island.

Continuing the journey westward through a region of undisputed richness and fertility of soil; past farms which have produced, thrice over, more than enough to make their owners independently rich, you scud by the unpretentious village of Hampton, and are shortly in sight of Middletown, a village whose marvellous growth, architectural beauty, progressiveness, and attractive surroundings have made it one of the most desirable places on the line of the Erie Railway, either for summer or permanent abode. The New York State Homœopathic Asylum for the Insane, of which a fine view is obtained as the train gracefully winds around the village, is here situated. Middletown is also the eastern terminus of the New York

Midland Railway and western terminus of the New Jersey Midland Railway.

Unless specially signalled, however, no stop is made at Middletown, the train speeding onward as if anticipating your long-cherished wish to view the Shawangunk range of mountains, which are clearly discernible as you approach Howell's. What a beautiful prospect! How it gladdens the eye, and calls into active being all of the human forces of imagination and admiration! A cultivated mountain with acres of woodland interspersed, and dotted here and there with pretty farmhouses! A patchwork of Nature than which no lovelier nor more enchanting could greet the human vision! But how is this vast mountain to be traversed? Is it a barrier to further progress? The train still moves, but its speed is somewhat arrested. The ascent of the mountain is being made gradually along its eastern slope, the grade averaging about sixty feet to the mile. Now you are at Otisville, and soon will have reached the summit, when the train, without any other power than its own weight, goes thundering along the western slope of the mountain, leaving Guymard behind, and bringing into full view Port Jervis, eight miles distant, with its church spires glittering in the sunlight, and the streams of the Delaware and Neversink, which here converge, reflecting, mirror-like, the endless variety and beauty of scenery which is spread out before you. Of a truth Nature has been lavish of her resources in beautifying the Eastern Division of the Erie Railway. But there are still in store for you scenes more glowing and of greater grandeur than any which have yet been presented. Port Jervis is reached at noon, and being the terminus of the Eastern Division, a change of engines is rendered necessary. While this is being done, you step upon the platform of the depot or of the coach, and avail yourself of the limited time allowed to study the situation and the characteristics of the village. You are not weary—feel as though you never spent three hours more pleasantly than in the passage over the Eastern Division of the Erie Railway, and so, when the conductor cries "All aboard," you resume your seat in the palace-coach, and await with pleasing anticipation the views to be witnessed in your progress over the next, or what is known as the

DELAWARE DIVISION.

As the train moves away from the depot, you observe a number of passengers who have, as you suppose, been left behind, but on making inquiry of the conductor, you learn that they are going to Milford, in Pennsylvania, eight miles distant by carriage-road, or to Monticello or White Lake, two very popular summer resorts in Sullivan County, which are reached by a Branch railway from Port Jervis, 24 miles in length.

The train is now under full headway You have fairly

entered the region conspicuous for the diversity and magnificence of its scenery, when lo! a scene of transcendent beauty attracts and rivets your attention. Below is the Delaware, whose devious windings check its struggle to escape from its mountain-bound captivity; near at hand is the Delaware & Hudson Canal, alike tortuous in its windings, carrying to tidewater the products of this section; while farther on and above are the Palisades of the Delaware—mountains whose bold and rugged appearance no less than their wondrous height, seem to bid defiance to an invasion of their domain. Soon you emerge from this scene, passing Pond Eddy and Shohola, and in turn reach Lackawaxen, where the train stops. From this point a Branch railway extends to Hawley and Honesdale, penetrating the rich anthracite coal regions of Northeastern Pennsylvania.

After leaving Lackawaxen you continue to follow the course of the Delaware in its tortuous and picturesque windings among the mountains, and are ever greeted with new and charming scenes, at some places intensely interesting. At Callicoon, where the train next stops, a scene of remarkable beauty occurs, which is only equalled by that of the famous Starucca Viaduct, which you witness after leaving Hancock and Deposit, and when near Susquehanna, at which last-named station the train stops for dinner.

You have now arrived at Susquehanna, the terminus of the Delaware Division; have dined at the Company's eating-house, where you found the table unexceptionable, and the attendance all that could be desired; and the trip thus far having proved neither tiresome nor monotonous, but on the contrary full of excitement and interest, you cheerfully resume your place in the palace-coach, and await the signal of the conductor for the train to proceed. Meantime you catch a glimpse of the extensive repair-shops of the Company at Susquehanna, which furnish employment for a large force of mechanics and laborers, and also of a branch railway running south to Carbondale and the coal mines of Pennsylvania.

The conductor has signalled the engineer, the bell rings, and off speeds the train over the

SUSQUEHANNA DIVISION.

This Division is not so noted for its magnificent scenery as for the many flourishing and enterprising cities and towns which appear at frequent intervals. The country being rather thickly settled, the weird and rugged scenes have given way to the more quiet and cultivated; and it is this disparity between the scenery of the Delaware and that of the Susquehanna which lends additional enchantment to both.

Binghamton, where the train next stops, is a city of rapid growth, and is generally regarded as being one of

3

the handsomest and most progressive cities of its size in the country. Its railroad facilities are exceptionally good, offering communication with all parts. To the south runs the Delaware, Lackawanna and Western Railroad, through Scranton and the Delaware Water Gap; with the North it communicates directly through Syracuse, Utica, and Oswego, while to the east it has an outlet via the Albany and Susquehanna Railroad. In the immediate vicinity are many noted summer resorts—Cooperstown, Richfield Springs, Sharon Springs, and Trenton Falls, being the most prominent.

Owego, the next stopping-place, is a town of considerable note. A Branch of the Delaware, Lackawanna and Western Railroad connects it with Ithaca and Cayuga Lake, and the Southern Central Railroad affords it immediate connection with Auburn.

Waverly, the next station in order, is rendered conspicuous by reason of its excellent facilities for travel to Philadelphia and the South, and its connection with the bituminous coal-fields of Pennsylvania. The Lehigh Valley Railroad which intersects with the Erie at this point, furnishes a large and valuable traffic, and in return derives an equally large and lucrative business from the Erie. From Waverly there is also connection with Ithaca and Geneva via the Geneva, Ithaca and Athens Railroad.

Elmira is next announced, and looking out of the car-window, you observe the sun sinking to rest. The whole horizon is lit up with its splendors of azure and gold ; the hillsides are tinged with ever-varying hues ; the valleys, the woodlands, the quiet country homes, all are bedecked in their evening array. Soon the scenes of beauty and interest, the panorama of constantly recurring changes which you have witnessed, will be enveloped in darkness. There are yet many views of absorbing interest on the route to Niagara Falls, and fixed in your resolution to make the entire journey by daylight, you pick up your satchel and other packages, and alight from the train when it stops at the dépôt. And in stopping at Elmira, you find yourself surrounded with all the advantages of larger cities. Next to Paterson it is the largest station on the line of the Erie Railway, and owing to its proximity to Havana and Watkins Glens, and its unrivalled railway facilities, it is decidedly the most desirable place at which to break your journey. The city itself has many attractions—Eldridge Park being the most widely known and generally visited.

After breakfasting next morning at an early hour, you are driven to the dépôt, and soon hear the whistle of an arriving express train. It is the Pacific Express, which left New York at 7 o'clock the previous evening, and will leave Elmira at 6 o'clock. Embarking on this train, which is almost wholly composed of sleeping and drawing-room coaches, you are soon in sight of Corning, the junction of the Rochester Division, over which there is a large travel to Avon Springs, and via Bath to Lake Keuka or Crooked Lake. There is also a branch road running southward from Corning to the coal-mines of Pennsylvania.

The train, after stopping at Corning, proceeds a few miles, when Addison is reached, and from here on to Hornellsville the road winds through a valley of picturesque beauty, watered by the Canisteo. At Hornellsville the train stops for breakfast at the Company's eating-house ; and while the passengers are making sad havoc of the good things here provided to appease their appetites, the coaches which are to run through to Cleveland, Cincinnati, and St. Louis, via the Atlantic and Great Western Railway, are detached from the train which is to go to Buffalo and Niagara Falls, and are removed to the track on the other side of the dépôt.

Breakfast over, the train is again in motion, and for some little distance runs parallel with the train directed for Cleveland, Cincinnati, St. Louis, and the Southwest. Soon they diverge, the one taking a southwesterly, and yours a northwesterly course. Now you have passed Arkport and Burns ; Canaseraga is sighted, and soon you will have arrived at Nunda, passing meanwhile the unpretentious stations of Garwood's and Swain's. In a few minutes you will be in the vicinity of Portage, and here you will witness one of the grandest views of which any country can boast. From the top of the bridge which spans the Genesee River at this point, and over which the cars pass, you are at an elevation of 234 feet above the river, whose tortuous windings you can distinctly trace for a distance of more than a mile, while beneath and around you are successively presented, in varying magnitude, rapids, pools, cataracts, cascades, and waterfalls. The entire scene is one of the utmost sublimity ; and as the train moves slowly away, shutting it out from sight, you pause to conjecture to what extent this region would be visited, could it, with all its manifold beauties, but be transferred to the environs of the metropolis.

At Gainesville an intersecting road leads to Silver Lake, a beautiful sheet of water on the wooded shores of which camp meeting and picnic grounds are located, besides a commodious hotel for tourists and summer boarders.

Onward moves the train, now stopping at Warsaw, now at Attica, and then at Buffalo. Here passengers for the West via the Lake Shore and Michigan Southern, Grand Trunk and Canada Southern railways, change cars, while those for Niagara Falls and the West, via the Great Western Railway of Canada, have yet an hour's ride before them ere will be disclosed to their vision the wonders of that world-famed creation of Divinity—NIAGARA FALLS!

It is one o'clock. You have arrived at Niagara Falls, and your journey is completed. You have traversed the entire length of the Erie Railway between New York and Niagara Falls (444 miles) by daylight; have passed through the beautiful valley of the Passaic; through the historic region of the Ramapo, and the rich dairy lands of Orange county; have crossed the Shawangunk range of mountains; been spellbound by the thrilling and interesting scenes of the upper Delaware region; have followed the meanderings of the Susquehanna, Chemung, and Canisteo rivers; have witnessed the rapids and falls of the Genesee river, and now, to crown all, you are face to face with the Falls of Niagara, commanding the most intense and awe-inspiring admiration of the observer. Although our artist has skilfully portrayed in the accompanying pages some of the principal features of this great wonder of nature, no representation or description can convey an adequate idea of the sublimity of the scene. The eye must see the great volume of rushing waters tearing over the rocks and tossing themselves into immense breakers, and hurrying madly towards the precipice over which they plunge into the seething basin of the Niagara 160 feet below; and the ear must hear the tremendous roar of the cataract—mingled as it is with the voice of the great Architect—in order to appreciate Niagara.

NUMBER OF MILES COMPRISING THE ERIE RAILWAY.

The Roads owned and operated by the Erie Railway Company are organized into Six General Divisions, and each General Division is subdivided as follows:

EASTERN DIVISION. Jersey City to Port Jervis, 88 miles; Jersey City to Paterson, via Newark, 19 miles; Jersey City to Nyack, 29 miles; Hackensack Junction to Spring Valley, 23 miles; Sufferns to Piermont, 18 miles; Turner's to Newburgh, 19 miles; Greycourt to Junction Newburgh Short Cut, 14 miles; Greycourt to Warwick, 10 miles; Goshen to Kingston, 43 miles; Goshen to Pine Island, 12 miles; Port Jervis to Monticello, 24 miles. Total miles Eastern Division and Branches, 299.

DELAWARE DIVISION. Port Jervis to Susquehanna, 104 miles; Lackawaxen to Honesdale, 25 miles; Susquehanna to Carbondale, 38 miles. Total miles Delaware Division and Branches, 167.

SUSQUEHANNA DIVISION. Susquehanna to Hornellsville, 140 miles. Total miles Susquehanna Division, 140.

ROCHESTER DIVISION. Corning to Rochester, 94 miles; Avon to Attica, 35 miles; Avon to Dansville, 30 miles. Total miles Rochester Division and Branches, 159.

BUFFALO DIVISION. Hornellsville to Buffalo, 91 miles; East Buffalo to Suspension Bridge, 23 miles. Total miles Buffalo Division and Branches, 114.

WESTERN DIVISION. Hornellsville to [...] miles; Carrollton to Gilesville, [...] mile Total [...] Western Division and Branches, 154.

Total miles Erie Railway and Branches on July 1874, 1,033.

THE WHIRLPOOL RAPIDS, NIAGARA RIVER, BELOW THE FALLS

"THROUGH BY DAYLIGHT" OVER THE ERIE RAILWAY.

CHARLES LEVER's vivid story of a "Ride for a Day," sprightly as it is in its narration of rapid travel, calls up no such enlivening picture as that which is furnished by a summer-day ride across New York State in the palace coaches of the Erie Railway. How all but incredible seems the accomplishment of such a journey in so brief a period! Yet the traveler after breakfasting in New York may take his seat in the Pullman Coach at the Erie Dépôt, and at supper time find himself in sight of the clear waters of Lake Erie, or within hearing of the thunders of Niagara's mighty cataract.

But more delightful than the mere achievement of such a victory over time and space, is the manner and method in which the feat is accomplished. For when such a glorious panorama is to be passed, no tourist intent upon seeing all that is beautiful and attractive in American scenery, will for a moment think of making his midsummer trip on the Erie Railway in any other time than in broad daylight. The train speeds over the landscape, along mountain sides, through valleys, over bridges, and across broad meadow lands with the speed of a winged charger, pausing only at long intervals, and then pushing on again farther than before, seemingly grudging its few lost moments of unavoidable delay. The traveler meanwhile ensconced in his cosy drawing-room or easy-chair, protected from dust and cinders, looks out upon the rapidly-

changing landscape with undisguised delight as in a varied
picture of town, city, hamlet, forest, and farm-land it passes
before him. Here, from amid all the luxurious surroundings of a first class hotel, he looks out alike upon nature's
wildest haunts and the cultivated homes of man, and wonders the while at the changes and improvements that
man's genius and energy have wrought. Hour after hour
brings him many miles nearer his goal, and lo! ere daylight has departed the wonderful journey has been accomplished. It has been to him one continued, unwearying
scene of entertainment and enjoyment, and his first word
of advice to his friend contemplating a tour eastward or
westward will be, as ours is, "Don't fail to enjoy, if you
can, a ride through by daylight over the Erie Railway."

THE SLEEPING AND DRAWING-ROOM COACHES OF THE ERIE RAILWAY

THERE is no Railway Company in the country which
provides better accommodations for its patrons, or which
keeps its passenger equipment in better condition, than
the Erie Railway.

The Drawing-room and Sleeping Coaches which are
attached to Express trains, both west and east, are, as is
shown in the illustrations given, perfect paragons of beauty
and models of comfort and luxury.

Indeed, the entire passenger equipment of the Erie
Railway is unsurpassed, and contributes in no small de-
gree to the wonderful growth and increase of its passenger
traffic.

brate some one or another festival occasion—some picnic, anniversary, or excursion, which ever it may be.

Yes, rural groves are in demand, and the Erie Railway Company, with the foresight characterizing it in its provisions for public accommodation, has undertaken to supply them by establishing, at convenient intervals along its route, shaded grounds enclosed and provided with tables, benches, and all other facilities for the convenience of Sunday-school or other picnic parties from the adjacent towns and villages. Swings and other attractions for the juvenile mind will be put up wherever practicable, boats will be provided for aquatic enjoyment, the grounds will be kept in perfect order, and, in short, everything will be done to render each of these groves a Paradise for picnic-goers. The step is a new and a good one, and is destined to prove annually a source of benefit to thousands of tired city-workers.

CHAUTAUQUA LAKE.

THIS charming body of water, eighteen miles long, and varying from one to three in width, is the farthest west of the many beautiful lakes which stud the surface of the Empire State, "the eyes of its landscape," as a poet has happily termed them. Chautauqua signifies, in the Indian dialect, "a foggy place," a term derived in this instance from the mist which frequently floats over its surface. The Erie Railway skirts the Lake's southern border, and from the car windows the passenger looks directly out upon its waters: at times placid as Lake Constance, at others lashed into fury with white caps. Lake Chautauqua is said to be the highest navigable water on the American continent, being 730 feet above Lake Erie, and 1,290 feet higher than the Atlantic Ocean. Steamboats run from Mayville, a beautiful and popular place of resort, at its northern extremity, to its southern outlet, whence small boats can descend to the Alleghany River.

EXCURSION AND PICNIC GROVES ON THE ERIE RAILWAY.

THE ancient Druids, however we may differ from them in our modern creeds, certainly had one good point in their worship—they chose the oak groves for their temples, and under those leafy shades celebrated their mystic rites. Now, while Druids are scarce to-day, nevertheless certain it is that this one excellent feature of their religion has been sedulously preserved, and as a proof of it we find, every summer, thousands of men, women and children inquiring for convenient groves in which to meet and cele-

IT may interest many readers to learn that while in Pennsylvania and other states there are no lakes of prominence, there are in the state of New York, on and near the line of the Erie Railway alone, no less than ten lakes, of which the following are most favorably known: Greenwood Lake, Orange Lake, Lake Mohonk, White Lake, Otsego Lake, Cayuga Lake, Seneca Lake, Lake Keuka, Silver Lake, and Chautauqua Lake.

TRAFFIC RESOURCES.

THE tourist, for profit as well as pleasure will note with surprise the number and variety of trains that continually throng the track, and will, perhaps, for the first time, realize how great is the volume of traffic in daily transit, and how complete and thorough must be the organization that can handle it with promptitude and despatch. Cars laden with live stock, coal, lumber, petroleum, ore, iron, and every conceivable form of manufacture and merchandise, pass in apparently exhaustless numbers, and justify the statement that places the Erie Railway, in respect to the magnitude of its tonnage traffic, foremost among the great Trunk Lines of the country.

It would be deeply interesting to trace the steady growth of its business from small beginnings to its present enormous proportions. Suffice it to say that the policy of the Company has ever been to develop the various mineral and agricultural resources of its line and branches, and to encourage the establishment thereon of large and important manufacturing industries. And recognizing the gratifying results of the past, its aim will be in the future to devise still more liberal arrangements, and to use every effort to attract new enterprises and foster those already in existence. To this end the transportation of materials for new manufacturing establishments will be done at about cost, and low special rates will be made for the shipment of the articles which they produce.

MINERAL RESOURCES ALONG THE ERIE RAILWAY.

A CURSORY survey of the route of the Erie Railway shows that the limestone necessary for use in smelting ores is found in abundance and of superior quality.

Large deposits of magnetic iron ores have been recently discovered on the Canada shore of Lake Ontario, a region for which the Erie Railway is one of the most available outlets to the coast. The yield of iron is reported as 65 to 75 per cent, and of a quality as rich as the ores of Iron Mountain, Missouri, which are in constant demand. Deposits of red fossiliferous ores, yielding 45 to 50 per cent, have also been found near Rochester, and extending thence for at least fifty miles eastward.

The Sterling Iron Mines, where the first iron works in America were established in 1751 by Lord Sterling, are but nine miles distant from the Erie Railway, and connected with it by a spur or branch road. Some three hundred tons of ore are shipped from these mines daily.

The entire Shawangunk range, which the Erie surmounts at the western end of its Eastern Division, about eighty miles from New York, is also said by experts to be rich in rare varieties of ores.

These various mineral resources, located on or contiguous to the line of the Erie Railway, are gradually building up extensive industries along the line, and promise before long to add largely to its local activities and its through traffic. "Each iron furnace, rolling mill, foundry, or manufacturing establishment," justly says a writer on this subject, "attracts to it an aggregate of population, through whose travel, and for the transportation of whose supplies and products, large sums of money are annually paid to carriers."

ERIE AND THE COAL FIELDS

WITHIN the past five years the coal traffic of the Erie Railway has assumed a vast and a constantly increasing importance. The branches or spurs running from the main line at Lackawaxen, Waverly, and Corning, respectively, into the heart of the great anthracite and bituminous coal-fields of Pennsylvania afford an easy and rapid egress for the carboniferous products of those regions to tide-water, and furnish alone a traffic sufficient to make the revenues of a kingdom, while in turn bringing to the inhabitants of those sterile, non-agricultural sections the cereals and provisions of the West at cheap and abundant rates.

The location of the Erie Railway is peculiarly favorable to this traffic, it being the first and only great line north of the coal-fields communicating directly with the seaboard on the one hand, and with the great West and the Canadas on the other. From the Wyoming fields in Luzerne County, for instance, it is but 114 miles via the Erie Railway to tide-water at Newburgh, as compared with 175 miles by the New Jersey Central and Lehigh Valley route, and 149 miles by that of the Delaware, Lackawanna, and Western to tide-water at New York. A considerable similar difference in distance exists in favor of the Erie over other roads in the connection with Buffalo and other Western points. The demand for anthracite coal in the West is a constantly increasing one, entering annually into a larger area of domestic and industrial uses. Its consumption at Cleveland alone, increased from 1,108 tons delivered by the Atlantic & Great Western Railroad in 1870, to 17,385 tons delivered by the same Company in 1872; and the ratio of increase has presumably been the same elsewhere. With such an immense field as this to supply, the future possibilities of this traffic, now only in its infancy, are almost without limit.

Of the eastward coal trade the same may be said, save that it is older and more developed. True, there is less domestic area to be supplied, but it is more densely populated, and beyond it is the foreign commerce of the entire world. With such a market to supply, where can a limit be placed to the demand? No supply, however great, can meet or interrupt it.

To confirm the justice of these statements with regard to the future of the Erie Railway's coal trade, a few figures may be cited, showing that in 1871 it aggregated in amount 2,199,418 tons; in 1872, 2,989, 680 tons, and in 1873, 3,994,832 tons. The statistics for the current year ending September 30, 1874, cannot yet of course, be presented, though showing thus far the same ratio of increase. But when we consider the growth as already shown, the inexhaustible supply on the one hand, and the increasing demand on the other, and the facilities and capacity afforded for its transportation, there can remain but little doubt that within five years *the aggregate coal tonnage of the Erie Railway will equal that of any other railway in the country.*

PETROLEUM.

THE attention of travelers will be inevitably drawn to the peculiar tank cars in which the crude oil is shipped. The trade itself is worthy of notice from its magnitude and regularity, and from the fact that the Erie Railway has at Weehawken, opposite New York, the most complete and extensive oil dépôt and docks in the country. From twelve to twenty vessels at a time may be seen at these docks loading with export oil. Last year new tankage capacity for 30,000 barrels was supplied to accommodate the rapidly increasing traffic.

Light and oil, illumination and lubrication, are prime necessities of modern civilization, and as petroleum combines in itself these essential qualities, it seems destined to supplant all other articles for lubricating purposes, and to become, outside of large cities, the general illuminator of the race. Since its introduction, gas works have been closed in many places, the manufacture of shale oil has been practically stopped in England, and the whaling interests of New England ports have been nearly ruined.

The Pennsylvania oil regions, which in 1872 furnished 88 per cent. of the entire production, are directly tributary to the Erie Railway. The production here has increased from *four* millions of gallons in 1859 to *four hundred* millions of gallons in 1872.

LIVE STOCK.

THE New York Statistical Annual closes its review of the live-stock market for 1872 with this remark : " Twelve million head of live-stock per annum will soon be required at the seaboard." The Erie Railway is making strenuous efforts to secure a fair proportion of this important source of revenue. Its stock-cars are of extra width ; its stock-trains are first class, with rights of passenger trains, and subordinate alone to them ; a special line telegraph runs from station to station, by means of which drovers are posted as to markets ; superior yards are established at

Oak Cliff on the Hudson, opposite New York, and in connection with them a new abattoir of the largest capacity and most complete appointment has just been finished. Commodious yards are located at Buffalo, ample grounds have recently been purchased at Suspension Bridge, and good feeding and watering yards are established along the line. By these and other inducements the Erie Railway Company is determined to maintain the reputation which its line has already gained of being the best stock-route in the country.

LUMBER TRAFFIC OF THE ERIE RAILWAY.

THE gradual clearing away of the forests in the Atlantic states annually renders the market more and more dependent upon the apparently inexhaustible supplies of the pine forests in the Saginaw region of Michigan, and the black walnut growths of Ohio and Indiana. These regions are directly tributary to the Erie Railway, and are annually shipping larger quantities of their precious products by it to the seaboard. Add to these the immense shipments of barrel staves from various Western sources to the East, and the extensive production of hemlock timber along the upper Delaware and its tributaries, and one may readily see that from this traffic alone the Erie Railway reaps annually an immense and constantly increasing revenue.

MILK TRAFFIC ON THE ERIE RAILWAY.

As has been elsewhere stated, the Erie Railway, within sixty miles of New York, passes through one of the finest dairy regions in America, the far-famed agricultural section of Orange County. As may be inferred, therefore, its daily milk traffic with the metropolis is no inconsiderable item of its daily receipts. In fact the extent of this business, and the perfect system to which it has been reduced, in order to facilitate the easy passage of the milk from the producer in the country to the consumer in the metropolis, would perhaps surprise the uninitiated. The cows are milked at a certain time every evening ; punctually, too, at a certain hour the farmer drives up with his twenty, thirty, or fifty cans to the station platform ; along comes the daily milk train ; in a moment or two the brimming cans are shipped, and away the train goes on to the next station. Midnight sees it rumbling into the dépôt at Jersey City, where scores upon scores of milk wagons, on each of which is inscribed "Pure Orange County Milk," are in waiting to receive their consignments of the creamy fluid, carry it across the river, and commence their matin rounds to supply the now slumbering denizens of the great city. So, day after day, year in and year out, New York is supplied with Orange County Milk by the thousands of gallons, and the traffic is constantly on the increase. Roads leading to the various stations have been improved, new platforms erected, and every facility for easy and rapid shipment afforded the farmer. As a consequence the annual trade increased from 6,180,537 gallons in 1862 to 11,721,481 gallons in 1872, or nearly doubled in ten years' time. At such a rate of increase, it is not difficult to foresee what the revenues, already immense from this source, are ultimately destined to become.

BUTTER, EGG, AND CHEESE TRAFFIC OF THE ERIE

LET us not despise the day of small things. "Many a mickle makes a muckle," and many a pound of butter, barrel of eggs, and package of cheese annually brings a mint of money to the Erie Railway's coffers. For instance, the receipts of butter at New York, in 1872, amounted to 49,651,770 pounds; of eggs, to 34,876,520 dozen; and of cheese to 99,713,820 pounds. The line of the Erie Railway seems to afford superior advantages to this class of products, and it has been, and still is, the effort of the Company to protect and increase them to the extent of its ability.

INCREASE OF MANUFACTURES.

STATISTICAL tables, carefully compiled in 1865 and 1873, show a most astonishing and gratifying increase in the number of manufacturing establishments on the Erie Railway during the brief intervening period. The most important of these are given in the following table:

MANUFACTURES.	1865	1873	INCREASE
Agricultural Implements	20	38	18
Blast Furnaces and Forges	15	35	20
Builders' Materials	64	167	103
Boiler, Car, and Locomotive Works	22	48	26
Brass and Iron Foundries	92	118	26
Breweries and Distilleries	135	197	62
Brush, Broom, and Carpet Factories	14	33	19
Cabinet Ware and Furniture Factories	59	111	52
Cooperage and Barrel Factories	54	94	40
Cheese Factories	18	72	54
Flouring and Grist Mills	151	184	33
Glass Works	4	10	6
Iron Railing and Fencing	30	45	15
Machine Shops	35	88	53
Marble Works	24	34	10
Nurseries	47	52	5
Oil Refineries	9	13	4
Planing Mills and Lumber Factories	104	204	100
Paper Mills	14	23	9
Piano and Musical Instruments	8	17	9
Soap and Candle	28	32	4
Saw and Shingle Mills	240	350	110
Silk Factories	14	31	17
Sugar Refineries	1	3	2
Tanneries	89	146	57
Varnish Factories	1	15	14
Vinegar Factories	9	16	7
Woollen Mills	12	18	6
Wagon and Carriage Factories	74	147	73
Miscellaneous	315	1022	707
Total	1702	3363	1661

4

THE PASSENGER TRAFFIC OF THE ERIE RAIL-WAY

THE following remarks and accompanying statement are copied from the "American Railroad Manual" of 1874, just published.

"In examining carefully the details of annual statement for year ending September 30, 1873, the reader cannot fail to be struck with the large percentage of increase in the passenger business on the Erie Railway, as compared with that of the other trunk lines which are its competitors for business. The appended statement will indicate very clearly the force of these remarks; and it will be further noted, by reference to the comparative statement of the source and movement of traffic, that the increase resulted mainly from *through*, and therefore competitive traffic."

Comparative Statement of Passenger Earnings of the Erie, Pennsylvania, New York Central, and Baltimore and Ohio Railways, for Fiscal Years 1872 and 1873.

NAME OF ROAD	Fiscal Year Each.	Passenger Mileages End of Year 1872.	Passenger Mileages End of Year 1873.	Increase for 1873.	Average per mileage of Total. Decrease 1873.
Erie	Sept. 30	$3,320,340	$3,595,538	$275,197	8.28
Pennsylvania Main Line	Dec. 31	4,202,502	4,350,612	148,110	3.52
New York Central	Sept. 30	2,203,003	2,538,446	335,443	15.22
Baltimore and Ohio	Sept. 30	2,154,934	2,255,058	100,124	4.64

As gratifying as this increase of business must be to the Managers of the Erie Railway, it is not unreasonable to assume that within the next two years the revenue from passenger traffic will exceed $5,000,000 per annum.

PORTAGE FALLS AND BRIDGE

To view this wondrous commingling of art and nature one were enough to invite the tourist to travel over the 362 miles which intervene between it and the Metropolis. Here the railway spans a gorge with perpendicular walls, through which the Genesee River leaps in three successive falls to the level of the valley below. The bridge by which it accomplishes this feat (see engraving) cost $175,000, and is the largest of its kind in the world. It stands upon thirteen stone-piers set in the river-bed, and sufficiently above high-water mark to be secure against freshets. Upon these piers the bridge rises 234 feet, and upon the top of this the railway track is laid. The bridge is 800 feet long, and so ingeniously constructed that any single timber in it can be removed and replaced at pleasure.

Symmetrical as is this imposing structure, it only serves to invest with a greater beauty and grandeur the natural scenery around it, for in some places the walls of the ravine which it spans are nearly 400 feet in perpendicular height, and the traveler looks down upon a dizzy view of the canal and the river, each passing through it on a different level below. But the view from below is immeasurably finer. Each of the three falls is well worth seeing. The upper, or Horseshoe Falls, are about seventy feet high. The Middle Falls, about a quarter of a mile farther down, pour into a chasm 110 feet below. A cave called the "Devil's Oven" has been worn into the rocks near the bottom of this fall. For a distance of two miles beyond this point the river winds through perpendicular walls of rock, then takes a series of rocky steps like a stairway, disappears for a moment under a shelving rock, and descends into a narrow pass about fifteen feet in width. Falling here twenty feet, it is

whirled back, and, turning abruptly off, falls again into a deep pool overshadowed by shelving rocks.

Two watchmen are kept on the bridge day and night, to put out any sparks which may fall from locomotives; and trains are run at a reduced rate of speed while crossing it, in order to give passengers an opportunity of enjoying the scenery of the valley below. All who have time should stop at the station near by, and spend a few hours in a drive to the different falls, or in a ramble along the banks of the river and canal.

A poetic mind naturally compares this valley, charming, with its high banks and walls, waterfalls and cascades, and distant fields covered with luxuriant verdure, to the Falls of Niagara, majestic only in mighty waters.

A description, however vivid, will afford the reader but a comparative idea of the grandeur and beauty of Portage Falls. To appreciate, one must see them, and let his own senses describe them for him.

ERIE'S COMBINATION WITH THE OCEAN STEAM-SHIP COMPANIES.

AWAKENED to the necessity for providing increased facilities for Immigrants landing at the port of New York, and with a view also to maintaining the admitted supremacy of the port of New York over all other American and Canadian seaports, the Erie Railway Company some months since entered into an alliance with the principal lines of ocean steamships, known as the "North Atlantic Conference," under which an entire change in the system of booking and forwarding Immigrant passengers from Liverpool and all parts of Europe and the Continent to the United States was effected. Previous to the formation of this compact it had been the custom of the Ocean Steamship Companies whose interests were identified with the port of New York, to book their Immigrant passengers to New York only, leaving it to the railways leading out of New York to furnish the necessary facilities for their transportation to their future homes in the great West. Under this policy, which had been prevalent for a number of years, and which was likely to continue had not the wisdom and forethought of the managers of the Erie Railway Company instituted a change, a portion of the immigration to the United States was being diverted from the port of New York to other unnatural and inferior American and Canadian ports.

This was accomplished by the adoption of a tariff of Immigrant rates, which, when added to the Ocean Steamship fare, made the through rates from Liverpool, &c., via Baltimore, Philadelphia, and Quebec, to Chicago and the West, from $1 00 to $3 00 less than via New York. The operations of this tariff, which discriminated against the port of New York and in favor of the ports above-named, were injurious alike to the City and State of New York, and to the steamship and railroad interests with whose prosperity New York heartily identifies itself. When, however, the managers of the Erie Railway perfected and concluded negotiations with the Ocean Steamship Lines, the disadvantages under which the port of New York had for years been laboring, and which threatened to seriously impair its commercial importance, were removed ; the system of booking and forwarding Immigrants was radically changed, so that now Immigrants may purchase through steamship and railway passage tickets in Liverpool or any part of Europe and the Continent to any part of the United States, at the same or even lower rates via New York than via any other American or Canadian seaport. And when the Immigrant lands at the port of New York and is transferred to the care and custody of the Erie Railway Company, he finds that a wise provision has thrown about him every safeguard for his protection and immunity from imposition. He finds safe and comfortable quarters at Castle Garden, surrounded by an attractive park of several acres beautifully laid out and thickly studded with shade-trees, and overlooking the bay and environs of New York. Here, both himself and family may remain until they shall have recovered from the fatigue consequent upon an ocean voyage ; and when prepared to resume the journey to their prospective homes in the West, the Erie Railway Company will transfer them by barge, free of charge, from Castle Garden to the Railway Dépôt in Jersey City, opposite New York, and thence to whatever part of the West they may have purchased tickets.

With a railway company whose managers seem so thoroughly to understand and appreciate the requirements of the Immigrant traffic, and through whose efforts so great a revolution has been brought about in the interest of the Immigrant as to enable him to secure passage as cheaply via the port of New York as via any other, it is not to be wondered at that the managers of the Ocean Steamship Lines cheerfully allied themselves ; and in so doing restored and re-established a hitherto prosperous business, and re-asserted the commercial importance and supremacy of the port of New York over all others.

THE FORWARDING OF IMMIGRANTS FROM CASTLE GARDEN TO THE WEST.

THE Immigrant coming to our shores and landing at the port of New York, no longer finds himself the prey of unscrupulous persons, but, on the contrary, is protected from every form of imposition.

On his arrival in the harbor of New York, directly opposite Castle Garden, the Immigrant comes under the charge of the Commissioners of Emigration, who provide for his transfer and that of his luggage, from the steamer to Castle Garden Dépôt.

Here he is conducted to the rotunda of the building, and registers his name, age, nationality, &c. If he has friends awaiting him, he is given over into their charge ; if he has money which he desires exchanged, the exchange is made at the rates current in Wall street ; if he has letters which he desires posted, the service is performed ; if he wishes to make any purchases of food, he can do so, at reasonable prices, within the enclosure of Castle Garden ; if he feels fatigued from the ocean voyage, and requires a few days' rest, he can remain within the Garden free of expense ; if he desires to take passage at once to the West, he can purchase his railroad tickets at the office of the Erie Railway in Castle Garden, at which office he can also have his luggage checked to destination.

He is then conducted to the barge of the Erie Railway, which is anchored alongside the Castle Garden pier, and when the hour arrives for the departure of the Immigrant Express train, he is transferred to the dépôt of the Erie Railway Company free of expense.

THE INDIAN RESER-
VATION.

On the Western Division of the Erie Railway, extending from Vandalia to Salamanca, is a vivid reminder of the fact that not over a century ago these fertile fields and thickly-settled regions were owned and tenanted by savage aborigines; for directly on the line of the road, nay, even intersected by it, is the Indian Reservation, where twenty-five hundred of the descendants of the Seneca braves who once waged such bloody warfare against the pale face, now dwell in a state of comparative civilization, following the arts of peace. They are governed by a President, one William Nephew, and without the questionable aid of Peace Commissioners or traders, have become a respectable, peaceable, and well-organized community.

LITTLE GLEN IRIS FALLS—PORTAGE.

SILVER LAKE.

Among the many beautiful summer resorts in Western New York, few may be said to enjoy a larger popularity than Silver Lake, a beautiful sheet of water three miles and a half long and one mile wide, situated in Wyoming County, upon the highest ground in that section of the State. During the last season over twenty thousand visitors sought recreation and pleasure beside its clear waters and amid the fine groves which line its shores. The Silver Lake Railway, connecting with the Erie at Gainesville, skirts the easterly shore of the lake for a distance of seven miles, terminating at the village of Perry, one mile beyond which, or at the foot of the lake, is an attractive summer hotel known as Saxton's Silver Lake House. Just beyond, on a splendid site overlooking the lake, stands another large hotel newly completed, with wide verandahs and elegant interior appointments. The excellent fishing in the lake has always made it a favorite resort for sportsmen of the hook and line; pickerel, bass, and white-fish are plentiful, while sail and row boats and fishing-tackle are provided for the accommodation of those who desire them. There is also on the lake a pretty little excursion-steamer, capable of carrying one hundred passengers.

A quarter of a mile above, on the lake shore, the Genesee Conference of the Methodist Episcopal Church have twenty acres of grove, where their annual camp-meetings are held. The grounds have been laid out in lots for the erection of cottages in which clergymen and others may spend the heated term, blending religious duties with social and rational enjoyment.

* * *

CROOKED LAKE.

This lake, situated partly in Steuben and partly in Yates County, New York is a pleasant summer retreat, and is reached by stages from Bath, on the Rochester Division of the Erie Railway. It is about twenty-two miles long and one broad, and derives its name from the fact that at its northern end it is divided by a beautiful wooded promontory into two forks, one five and the other about nine miles long. It is also sometimes spoken of under the more modern title of Keuka Lake. Grape-growing is extensively carried on along its shores, which are remarkable, it may be also stated, for their picturesque scenery. Two steamers ply from Penn Yan at its foot to Hammondsport on the south end of the lake, and the trip in summer-time is a delightful one.

Commodious hotels may be found at Penn Yan and Hammondsport, and at Grove Spring, on the east side of the lake, a large building has been erected as a summer resort, where visitors are afforded every means of enjoyment.

* * *

The Erie Railway has been fortunate in the titles given to some of the beautiful landscapes along its line. In a day's ride one may see Ramapo Valley, the American Switzerland—"a title which was first applied to the Ramapo Pass of New York by N. P. Willis, and which has since been given in turn to every spot found charming by enterprising tourists"—Starucca Valley, "the Yo-Semite of the East," celebrated in Cropsey's picture of an American autumn scene and the incomparable Niagara Falls.

AMERICAN FALLS FROM BELOW

NIAGARA FALLS.

THE Niagara River, the strait or link connecting the two great lakes, Erie and Ontario, though but thirty-four miles long, yet passes in that brief space through a tremendous struggle with the rock-ribbed battlements which line and traverse its current. In those thirty-four miles

it accomplishes a total descent of three hundred and thirty-four feet, fifty-one feet of which it descends in the space of three-quarters of a mile in the Rapids which mark its approach to the terrible leap of nearly two hundred feet more—the world-renowned Falls of Niagara.

Over this great cataract has been pouring ceaselessly through the centuries of the past, with the deafening roar of a thousand thunders, a torrent of water three-fourths of a mile wide and twenty feet in depth, or an aggregate, it is calculated, of a hundred millions of tons per hour. No wonder that to this grandest of natural shrines the untutored aborigines were wont to come yearly to worship their Great Spirit, and propitiate him by the sacrifice of an Indian maiden, sent down on the current in a flower-laden canoe to her death in the terrible vortex; no wonder that they led thither the first missionaries who penetrated these wilds, and pointed in speechless awe to the mighty cataract; and no wonder that in these later days thousands and thousands of tourists from every part of this country and Europe annually make this spot their destination, and stand gazing in mute surprise, as did the savage and the priest before them, at this wonder of the world!

From the American side of the Falls the visitor has access to the various rocky islands—Goat, Chapin's, Luna, and the Three Sisters—which break the face of the Falls, and enable him to overlook its very brink midway in the river's current. From this side, too, he descends to the Cave of the Winds, and may visit the Whirlpool Chasm Tower, and the Devil's Hole.

From the Canada side, opposite, which is reached by a wire suspension-bridge 1,268 feet long, may be viewed the magnificent sweep of the Cataract known as the Horseshoe Fall, (1,900 feet across,) the Burning Spring, the historic village of Chippewa, and the battle-field of Lundy's Lane. Or, by a railroad running on an inclined-plane, from a point on the American side near the brink of the Cataract, the visitor may descend to the river directly below the Falls, and looking upward at them from the deck of the ferry-boat which plies from shore to shore, may more than before realize the immensity and grandeur of the scene. It will leave in his memory an impression and sense of admiration that a lifetime will not serve to eradicate.

The hotels at Niagara Falls are large, numerous, and well conducted. Great precautions are now taken by the authorities to insure every convenience to sightseers, and to prevent extortions and impositions of every kind.

PROSPECT POINT—NIAGARA FALLS

BLOOMING GROVE PARK

UNDER this rather unpretentious title there exists in Northeastern Pennsylvania, close upon the line of the Erie Railway, a grand forest park of seven hundred acres, enclosed with a wire fence, and embracing within its limits almost every conceivable surface formation in hills, mountains, valleys, and undulating plateaux. Its forests include the oak, the hemlock, the chestnut, beech, spruce, cedar, maple, birch, pine, hickory, butternut, and other varieties of trees. The enclosure is irregular in shape, having been so laid out as to include the finest lakes and streams. By this arrangement the park, in addition to many miles of fine trout brooks, has within its limits no less than eight fresh-water lakes, the largest nearly three miles in circumference, and all with waters clear as crystal, and teeming with black bass and a variety of fish common to our lakes.

"What a tempting resort for the angler!" the reader will exclaim. Yes, and for the hunter and sportsman too. For upon these lands are to be found the black bear, wildcat, otter, mink, fox, coon, marmot, deer, and several varieties of squirrels and hares. The birds include the eagle, hawk, owl, blackbird, woodcock, bluebird, several varieties of duck, partridge, mountain finch, pigeons, quail, the loon, and other migratory birds. Ruffled grouse, woodcock, and deer, are especially numerous, and additions to the stock are constantly being made. Engagements have been closed with hunters in various parts of the country, and with army officers on the frontier, to forward moose, elk, deer, antelope, Rocky Mountain sheep and goats, and other animals. Some English pheasants and a few wild turkeys have been set at liberty in the Park.

The Association owning the Park may be said, in general terms, to have for its object the fuller development of field and aquatic sports. It is composed of a number of wealthy gentlemen, principally New-Yorkers, who hold a valuable charter from the state of Pennsylvania, and already own about twelve thousand acres of land, as well as several thousand adjoining acres leased in addition, of which, as previously stated, about seven hundred acres are already enclosed with wire. Suitable provisions, by means of dogs and keepers, are made against poaching, and heavy penalties are provided for the punishment of offenders.

The accessibility of the Park to New York, being only about twelve miles distant from Lackawaxen, or four hours' ride via the Erie Railway, makes it a convenient place of resort for members of the Association, their families, and invited guests, who here find every variety of enjoyment, while experiencing the benefits resulting from the healthfulness of the locality.

CONNECTIONS OF THE ERIE RAILWAY.

FROM various points on the Erie Railway, extending, as it does, from the Hudson to Lake Erie and the Ohio River, and traversing regions in which are successively represented every variety of natural resources, diverge connecting lines, which may not inaptly be designated the vertebræ, of which the Erie is the spinal column. Let us glance briefly at these, and at the regions to which they lead us.

At Middletown the Erie connects with the New York and Oswego Midland Railway, recently opened through to Oswego, the greatest grain emporium on Lake Ontario. At Lackawaxen, diverges the Honesdale Branch, running directly into the heart of the Pennsylvania coal region. At Binghamton, three tributary roads come in—the Albany and Susquehanna, extending to Albany, the state Capital; the Syracuse and Binghamton Railroad, extending to Syracuse and Oswego, and the Delaware, Lackawanna and Western Railroad, coming in from Scranton and the South, and running to Utica. At Owego a branch of the latter road also diverges to Ithaca, the seat of Cornell University, and the Southern Central Railroad connects for Auburn. At Waverly comes in the great Lehigh Valley Railway, extending from Easton, and forming in connection with the North Pennsylvania Railroad, a favorite route between Philadelphia and Niagara Falls and the West. At Elmira, the Northern Central Railroad, running north and south, intersects the Erie. Here also come in the Chemung Canal, connecting with Seneca Lake, and the Junction Canal, leading southward to the coal fields. At Corning diverges the Blossburg Railroad, and running northward is the Rochester Division. At Hornellsville the main line divides into two great forks or branches, the one running to Buffalo and Niagara Falls, and the other to Salamanca and Dunkirk. At Salamanca connection is made with the Atlantic and Great Western Division, extending to Cincinnati and Cleveland. At Dunkirk connection is made with the Lake Shore and Michigan Southern Railway. At Buffalo, the trains of the Erie Railway connect with those of the Lake Shore & Michigan Southern, Grand Trunk and Canada Southern Railways. At Suspension Bridge, connection is made with the Great Western & Michigan Central Railway.

The Erie Railway, it will thus be seen, lays under direct tribute to itself, an immense area of country, embracing, to a greater or less extent, the entire grain-producing regions of the West. Navigable rivers and canals, connecting railroads and inland lakes, all vie in bringing to it an amount of freight and travel, which may well justify its being ranked among the most important of our national highways.

View of the Commodious Barge provided by the Erie Railway Company for the transfer of Emigrants and their Luggage from Castle Garden to the Erie Railway Depot.

MAP OF THE CITY OF NEW YORK

Showing the location of the Freight and Passenger Stations, Ferries, Street Car Lines, Offices, Terminal Facilities & Connections of the

ERIE RAILWAY
AND THE
OCEAN STEAMSHIP LINES.

REFERENCES

1 Erie Railway Passenger & Freight Depot, foot of Chambers St.
2 " " " Twenty-third St.
3 " " General Office, Twenty-third St. & Eighth Avenue.
4 " " Ticket & Freight Office, 957 Broadway, cor. of Twenty-third St.
5 " " " 529 " Spring St.
6 " " " 241 " opposite City Hall.
7 " Freight Pier, East River. 10 Cooper Institute.
8 " Ticket Office, 54 Hudson St., Hoboken. 11 Union Square.
9 Academy of Music. 12 Madison Square.

www.ingramcontent.com/pod-product-compliance
Lightning Source LLC
Chambersburg PA
CBHW021452090426
42739CB00009B/1727